Smoke Signals to Smartphones

Becca Heddle

Explorer Challenge

Find out how flags help us
to communicate …

OXFORD
UNIVERSITY PRESS

Contents

We Like to Talk!

Do you like to have a conversation? Most of us like to talk – and people have been chatting for thousands of years. All through history, people have also invented ways to send messages when they are far apart.

People have always used the latest technology to send messages – from cave paintings to signals through space. As time goes by, we have found faster and better ways of communicating than people had before us.

Messages from Prehistory

About 20 000 years ago, people did not know how to write. **Prehistoric** people could only make things using stone, animal parts, plants and fire. But they left communications that we can read now, in ancient paintings on cave walls.

Messages in Smoke

By 800 BCE, people sent messages between signal towers on the **Great Wall of China**, using smoke. Every tower's lookouts could see the next tower in each direction. They copied the smoke signals to pass the message on from tower to tower. The signals were for simple messages, such as warning of enemy attacks.

Smoke signals are still used today to send out a call for help.

Pigeon Post

Pigeons have an amazing ability to find their way home. People realized this around 3000 years ago. They started to send short messages by writing them down and fixing them to a pigeon's leg.

This is a messenger pigeon from World War I.

The message goes in here.

Dispatch Riders

By about 540 BCE, the rulers of **Persia** were using fast horses to send messages. Each **relay** rider would pass the message on to the next, until they reached the person the message was for.

This is a rider on the Pony Express. Horse relays were used to deliver messages across America in the 1860s.

Postal Systems

Long ago, very few people could read and write.
But by the 1600s, more people were learning.
Some countries set up official postal systems.
Anyone could use these to send letters.

The mail coach picked up letters from post offices and delivered them to other parts of the country.

POST OF

People had to pay postage for every sheet of paper they sent. So they tried to fit as much as they could on each page.

I'm turning the paper sideways and writing more in a different direction to fit more words on one page!

By 1830, letters had begun to travel by train in the United Kingdom. They could travel hundreds of miles and arrive the next day!

Flagging It Up

H   E   L   L   O

By the late 1700s, the French had developed a semaphore (*say* sem-a-for) system. This used towers with two wooden arms on top that could be moved into different positions. Each position was for a different word. From the mid-1800s, British ships used semaphore too. Two flags were held in different positions for each letter of the alphabet.

Morse Code

In the 1830s, Morse code was invented. It was a way of sending messages along electrical wires. You spelled out your message as long and short signals. At the other end of the wire, the signals came out as flashes, beeps or printed dots and dashes. Then someone could decode them to read the message.

message in Morse code

Telephones

early telephone

1950s telephone

The telephone was invented in 1876. For the first time, you could actually speak to someone who was miles away. You could hear their voice coming along the wire.

Mobile Phones

In 1973, a 'mobile' phone was invented – one which didn't need a wire. Ten years later, mobile phones cost about the same amount of money as a small car. By the 1990s, they were much cheaper and millions of people around the world owned one. By 2013, more people had a mobile phone than had a toilet.

Mobile phones mean people can make calls to and from almost anywhere in the world, even in places with no wires at all.

Computers

In the 1950s, computers were so big they took up whole rooms. By the 1980s, computers could be small enough to fit on desks and by the 1990s, it was common to have a computer at home.

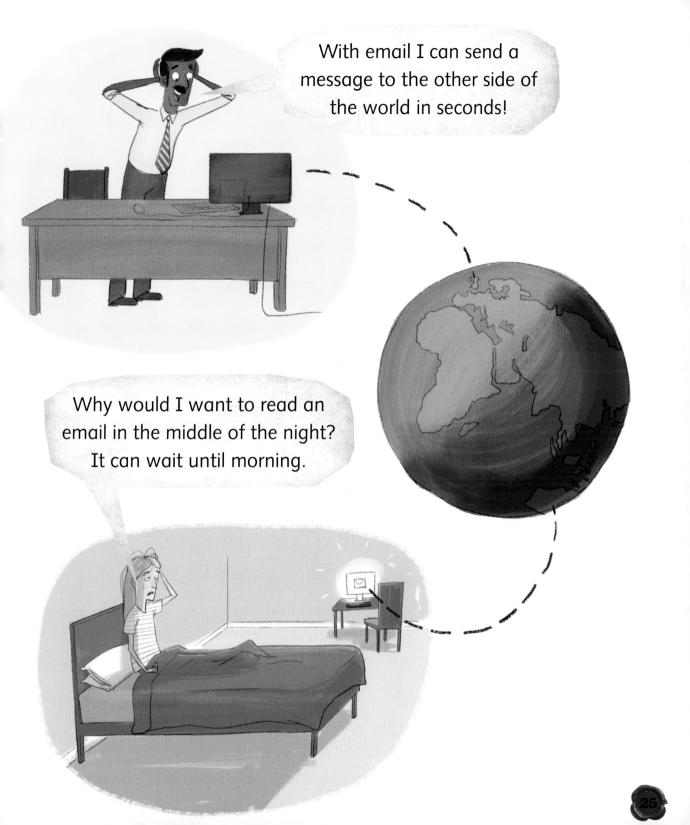

Smartphones

an early
smartphone

Smartphones started to become popular in 2007. Now people can have these tiny computers with them all the time. A single smartphone has more computing power than all of **NASA**'s computers had in the 1960s when they landed the first man on the moon.

What Next?

Human communications have come a long way, from cave paintings and smoke signals to video calls. What might the next developments look like? Might we be able to send computer messages straight to each other's brains?

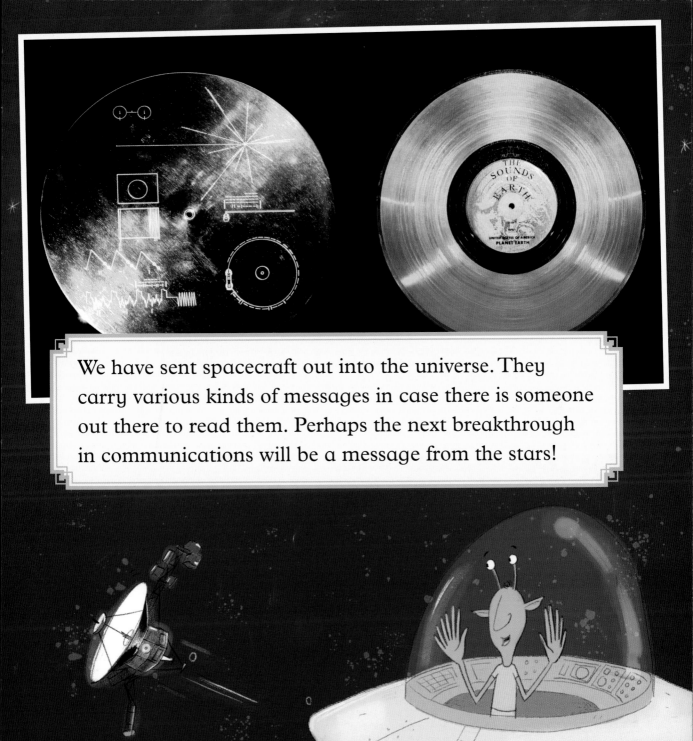

We have sent spacecraft out into the universe. They carry various kinds of messages in case there is someone out there to read them. Perhaps the next breakthrough in communications will be a message from the stars!

Glossary

Great Wall of China: a very long wall in China, built to keep invaders out

NASA: an American government agency that researches, develops and launches space flight

Persia: a large ancient kingdom centred around what is now the country of Iran

prehistoric: from ancient history, a time before written records were kept

relay: people or groups taking it in turns, with each one taking over from another

Index

Look Back, Explorers

How did people send messages using smoke signals on the Great Wall of China?

Why are mobile phones called 'mobile'?

Why would semaphore be tricky in bad weather?

What are the good and bad things about sending messages using a carrier pigeon?

Imagine you met a prehistoric person. What questions would you ask them? How would you try to communicate with them?

Did you find out how flags help us to communicate?

Explorer Challenge: semaphore flags are held in different positions for each letter of the alphabet (page 16)

What's Next, Explorers?

Now that you have read about lots of different ways to communicate, find out what happens when Biff, Chip and Nadim go on a magic key adventure and need to deliver an urgent message to a queen ...

Explorer Challenge
for *The Urgent Message*

Find out how this man is called to the Queen ...